To Honour Women`s Day

OFILES OF LEADING WOMEN IN THE SOUTH AFRICAN
D NAMIBIAN LIBERATION STRUGGLES

Sources and Abbreviations

Abbreviations used in the footnotes to this book are as follows:-

CT	—	*Cape Times*, Cape Town
Post	—	*Post*, Johannesburg (effectively banned end 1980)
Sechaba—		quarterly journal of the African National Congress (ANC)
S. Exp	—	*Sunday Express*, Johannesburg
T	—	*The Times*, London
Voice	—	*Voice*, Johannesburg
VOW	—	*Voice of Women*, journal of the ANC Women's Section

Besides the references quoted in the text, the following sources have been made use of in compiling the biographies:

IDAF *Information Service* 1967–1974

Focus on Political Repression in Southern Africa, IDAF News Bulletin, 1975 onwards

For their Triumphs and For their Tears — Women in Apartheid South Africa, by Hilda Bernstein, (IDAF, rev. ed. 1978)

From Protest to Challenge — A Documentary History of African Politics in South Africa 1882–1964, edited by Thomas Karis and Gwendolen M. Carter, vol. I (Hoover Institution Press, 1972)

Organize or Starve! The History of the South African Congress of Trade Unions, by Ken Luckhardt and Brenda Wall (Lawrence and Wishart, 1980)

Various United Nations publications, particularly those of the United Nations Centre against *Apartheid.*

(Where no sources are given, the material is taken from South African or other press reports.)

To Honour Women's Day

Profiles of leading women in the South African and Namibian liberation struggles

Fight for an Africa
where women are not slaves,
Fight for an Africa where women
do not waste their lives;
South Africa in fact
is on its way,
to celebrate its freedom
and to honour women's day.

(from *POETS TO THE PEOPLE*
'Women's Day Song')

International Defence and Aid Fund for Southern Africa
in co-operation with
United Nations Centre Against *Apartheid*
AUGUST 1981.

© INTERNATIONAL DEFENCE AND AID FUND

Published 1981

The International Defence and Aid Fund for Southern Africa is a humanitarian organisation which has worked consistently for peaceful and constructive solutions to the problems created by racial oppression in Southern Africa.

It sprang from Christian and humanist opposition to the evils and injustices of apartheid in South Africa. It is dedicated to the achievement of free, democratic, non-racial societies throughout Southern Africa.

The objects of the Fund are:–

(i) to aid, defend and rehabilitate the victims of unjust legislation and oppressive and arbitrary procedures,

(ii) to support their families and dependents,

(iii) to keep the conscience of the world alive to the issues at stake.

In accordance with these three objects, the Fund distributes its humanitarian aid to the victims of racial injustice without any discrimination on grounds of race, colour, religious or political affiliation. The only criterion is that of genuine need.

For many years, under clause (iii) of its objects, the Fund has run a comprehensive information service on affairs in Southern Africa. This includes visual documentation. It produces a regular news bulletin 'FOCUS' on Political Repression in Southern Africa, and publishes pamphlets and books on all aspects of life in Southern Africa.

The Fund prides itself on the strict accuracy of all its information.

This book was prepared by IDAF Research, Information and Publications Department

19 JAN 1982

ISBN No. 0 904759 46 6

Contents

Introduction

On 9 August 1956, 20,000 women from all over South Africa and representing a great variety of social backgrounds converged on the Union Buildings in Pretoria to see the Prime Minister of the apartheid regime. Many had come at great personal cost and in the face of concerted official obstruction. The issue which had brought them together was the regime's decision to extend the hated pass laws to women.

It was an historic and moving occasion:

"All processions in Pretoria were banned that day, so the women walked to Union Buildings to see the Prime Minister in groups of never more than three. All Pretoria was filled with women. This was four years before the national liberation organizations were banned, and thousands of women wore the green and black Congress blouses; Indian women dressed in brilliant saris; Xhosa women in their ochre robes with elaborate headscarves.

Union Buildings is designed in classic style, with pillared wings on either side of an amphitheatre on a hillside, with trees and gardens in steps down the hillside and a vista to the town far down below across a long avenue of lawn. The women slowly converged up this avenue and filled the amphitheatre. Their leaders went into Union Buildings and left hundreds of thousands of signatures on petition forms at the office of the Prime Minister who, of course, was not available to see them. Afterwards they stood in complete silence in the winter sun—even the babies on their backs did not cry—for thirty minutes, then burst into magnificent harmony to sing anthems, *Nkosi sikelel' iAfrika* and *Morena Boloka*. The singing, as they dispersed, echoed over the city, and the women began a new freedom song with its refrain Wathint' abafazi, wayithint' imbolodo uzokufa — 'Now you have touched the women you have struck a rock, you have dislodged a boulder, you will be crushed'."*

The 1956 demonstration shook the apartheid regime. It was impressive evidence of the power of angry but highly organized women and it marked an important stage in the growth of unity among all the oppressed. It represented, furthermore, the culmination of a period of concerted, countrywide mobilization and protest. In turn, the great march led to further determined struggle.

Over the years to follow, the South African government was to face increasingly daring and serious challenges. In Namibia, where it had since 1915 endeavoured to enforce its racial laws and practices in defiance of world opinion, the formation of the South West Africa People's Organization (SWAPO) in 1960 ushered in a phase of the liberation struggle which would by 1981 demand the deployment of 100,000 South African troops to retain apartheid's grip on the

---

4

For their Triumphs and For their Tears—Women in Apartheid South Africa, by Hilda Bernstein (IDAF 1978).

20,000 women gathered outside the Union Buildings in Pretoria on 9 August 1956.

illegally occupied territory. Here too, women were to play a crucial role as supporters, organizers and fighters of the national liberation movement and the armed struggle.

This book has been produced by the International Defence and Aid Fund for Southern Africa (IDAF) in co-operation with the United Nations Centre against *Apartheid*, as a tribute to the fighting women of South Africa and Namibia on the occasion of the 25th anniversary of the pass law protest and of South African Women's Day.

The women whose lives and experiences are briefly described in the following pages have all made outstanding contributions to the struggle for a free, democratic and non-racial Southern Africa. All have endured personal hardship and suffering under apartheid. They have been banned, detained, tortured, imprisoned, driven into exile or have experienced other forms of victimisation. In the climate of repression and war which characterises South Africa and Namibia today, hundreds of other women who in other circumstances would be obvious candidates for inclusion in a book of this kind, must remain anonymous. The risks both to themselves, and to families, friends and colleagues, which could be brought about by international publicity at a time when their energies and skills are actively deployed in ongoing struggles inside Southern Africa, are too great.

The biographies below have been selected not just as those of individuals, but as representative of all the women who, throughout South Africa and Namibia, are carrying forward the banner of the freedom struggle in the townships, the houses, farms and factories of their employers, the regime's prisons and detention camps, in the bantustans, and from places of exile throughout the world. This book is dedicated to them.

5

Key to National Women's Organizations in South Africa and Namibia

AFRICAN NATIONAL CONGRESS WOMEN'S LEAGUE (ANC WL)
was formed in 1919, seven years after the ANC was formed. The ANC WL was particularly active in organizing women in opposition to the pass laws. The Women's League was banned with the ANC in 1960. It is now constituted as the Women's Section of the ANC.

FEDERATION OF SOUTH AFRICAN WOMEN (FSAW)
was formed in 1954 in a spirit of unity and internationalism, by women in the Congress Alliance (particularly from the ANC WL), women's organizations and trade unions. It was launched under the slogan "Forward to freedom, security, equal rights and peace for all". The FSAW convened a provincial conference of women in 1955, at which the Women's Charter was adopted. The women's demands were ultimately incorporated in the Freedom Charter, adopted shortly afterwards at the Congress of the People in Kliptown. The FSAW was severely restricted in the early 1960s, largely because of the restrictions placed on the leadership by the regime, and particularly the banning of the ANC.

BLACK WOMEN'S FEDERATION (BWF)
was formed in December 1975 at a conference organized by a local Natal organization, the Black Women's Federation. 41 organizations were represented in the national BWF. Members of the BWF were united in their unconditional rejection of Bantu Education and full support of the Soweto students. Seven members, including four executive members, were detained between August and December 1976. The BWF itself was banned in October 1977.

WOMEN'S FEDERATION OF SOUTH AFRICA (WFSA)
was formed recently. Members are actively involved in struggles in opposition to the rent increases and Bantu Education, and played a major role in the campaign in 1981 to boycott the regime's celebrations of the 20th anniversary of its republic.

THE SWAPO WOMEN'S COUNCIL (SWC)
had its origins in a Consultative Congress held in Tanga, Tanzania in December 1969 by the South West Africa People's Organization (SWAPO) of Namibia. The Congress decided to establish a women's wing to mobilise, develop and deepen political consciousness among Namibian women and to bring about their active participation in the national liberation struggle. The SWC was formally inaugurated as a wing of SWAPO with its own constitution and secretariat in August 1976. The first Consultative Congress of the SWC took place at Roca Rio Goa, in the People's Republic of Angola, in January 1980. The SWC has undertaken educational work among women, set up health care, literacy schemes and agricultural cooperatives in SWAPO's refugee settlements in Angola and Zambia, and, inside Namibia, organized political meetings and raised funds to assist the families of political prisoners. Internationally, the SWC has forged working relationships with women's organizations in many countries.

Glossary of Important Dates and Events

Besides the pass law campaign, some other important dates and events from the recent history of the liberation struggle and mentioned in the biographies are:

1952 DEFIANCE CAMPAIGN AGAINST UNJUST LAWS
launched on 26 June 1952, South Africa Freedom Day, by the African National Congress (ANC) and the Indian Congress. More than 8,500 disciplined volunteers or "defiers" were imprisoned for peacefully refusing to obey apartheid laws. The campaign caught the imagination of the people and attracted thousands who became politically involved in the struggle.

1955 CONGRESS OF THE PEOPLE
held on 26 June 1955 at Kliptown, near Johannesburg. Jointly organized by the ANC, Indian Congress, Coloured People's Congress and the Congress of Democrats as a platform for the expression of the people's demands. Suggestions were collected at meetings held throughout the country and incorporated into the Freedom Charter which was adopted by the Congress while the police moved in and interrogated the delegates.

1956– TREASON TRIAL
1961 The regime regarded the Freedom Charter as High Treason and for 18 months after its adoption police raided homes to collect "evidence". On 6 December 1956, 156 men and women were arrested and charged with High Treason. The trial lasted until March 1961, when all the accused had been acquitted.

1960 STATE OF EMERGENCY
On 21 March 1960, 69 peaceful demonstrators were shot dead by the police in Sharpeville, Transvaal. Others were killed in Langa, Cape Town, shortly afterwards. In protest at the shootings, a one-day nation-wide strike was organized, during which thousands of Africans burnt their passes. The regime responded by declaring a national State of Emergency, arresting over 20,000 people and detaining a further 2,000 political activists for months without trial. The ANC and the Pan-Africanist Congress were both banned. The liberation struggle entered a new phase in which the organizations concluded that armed struggle was unavoidable.

South Africa

FRANCES BAARD

Frances Baard is one of the many women to contribute towards building a non-racial trade union movement in South Africa. Now aged over 80, she lives in a remote part of the Northern Transvaal following banishment for her political activities.

Born in 1901, she worked as a domestic servant and then a teacher and later became Secretary of the Food and Canning Workers Union, Port Elizabeth branch. She was active in trade union work throughout the 1950s and '60s. She frequently represented the food and canning workers on the Port Elizabeth Local Committee of the South African Congress of Trade Unions (SACTU) and attended SACTU Annual Conferences as their delegate. She was one of the few women on the SACTU National Executive.

Frances was also active in the political struggle. She joined the ANC in 1948 and was Secretary of the ANC Women's League in Port Elizabeth. She played a prominent part in the Federation of South African Women (FSAW) and took part in an extensive campaign against the pass laws in the Port Elizabeth area following the 1956 women's demonstration in Pretoria.

Frances participated in the 1952 Campaign of Defiance against Unjust Laws and in the boycott of Bantu Education in 1955. She was one of the ANC organizers arrested in 1956 and subsequently charged in the Treason Trial. From the dock she called on others:

"No matter where you work, unite against low wages . . . unite into an unbreakable solidarity and organization."*

In the 1960s she faced increasing periods of imprisonment as the state attempted to silence her. She was detained in December 1962 and then banned in January 1963. In 1963 she was again arrested and kept in solitary confinement for a year before her trial. She was then imprisoned for five years, sentenced under the Suppression of Communism Act. On her release in 1969 she was banished to Mabopane in the Northern Transvaal.

The ban has now been lifted, but she has remained in Mabopane as she no longer has a house in Port Elizabeth. Frances' children were evicted from the family home in Port Elizabeth when she was banned.

Organise or Starve by K. Luckhardt and B. Wall, Lawrence & Wishart, 1980.

Frances Baard.   Nkosazana Dlamini.   *Photo: Morning Star.*

Frances Baard (*wearing dark glasses*) with colleagues at a demonstration.

9

NKOSAZANA DLAMINI

While serving as the Vice-President of the South African Students' Organization (SASO), Nkosazana Dlamini was also an active underground member of the African National Congress. She left South Africa in September 1976, in the wake of the Soweto uprising, and has since completed her training as a medical doctor in exile.

Nkosazana was born in Pietermaritzburg in 1949. She lived with her family in Durban, and attended primary school there. She went to high school at Amanzimtoti training college, and secured her B.Sc. in zoology at the University of Zululand.

While studying at university, she came into contact with older people and made a number of white friends. Through personal experience of the difficulties of sustaining such friendships under apartheid, she became interested in knowing more about the intricacies of the South African system as well as its international connections.

When the Soweto uprising began in June 1976, Nkosazana was in her fifth year as a medical student at Wentworth, University of Natal, with just one year to go before becoming a fully qualified doctor. Events came to a head as the students were in the middle of their half-yearly exams, but together with others, she decided to continue with her political work.

"I knew that if it came to the crux, I would have to leave the country. But there was no point in leaving what I had started just for a degree. Even if I had passed the degree, I would still suffer the same oppression. It was a feeling, you know, that to make something of education—or anything else—there must be a complete political change."*

As a member of SASO, Nkosazana was involved in a number of community projects ranging from literacy to home industries, legal and medical aid. She and other medical students ran non-racial clinics in the Indian, African and Coloured ghettos.

She became an obvious target for the police through her prominence as SASO's Vice-President. When she finally left South Africa in September 1976, it was after weeks spent evading a police search by moving from room to room in the men's hostels of Natal University. On one occasion she had a narrow escape, being arrested and fined for trespassing. She evaded detection by giving a false name. At the time she escaped into exile, she was the only member of the SASO executive not in detention.

Following her arrival in Western Europe, Nkosazana became actively involved in political work with the ANC, giving interviews and addressing many meetings and conferences organised by anti-apartheid groups. She was also able to resume her interrupted professional career, and is now a practising doctor.

JANUB GOOL

A founder member of the Unity Movement of South Africa, Janub "Jane" Gool has been active in the liberation struggle for over 45 years. She fled South Africa in 1963 after playing a leading role in struggles against the extension of apartheid to the Coloured community, and now lives in exile.

Jane, her younger brother the late Dr. Goolam Gool, and I. B. Tabata, President of the Unity Movement, were founder members of the All-African Convention (AAC) in 1935. She became an executive member of the Anti-CAD (Coloured Affairs Department) Movement, a united front of mainly Coloured organizations formed to fight against the establishment of an apartheid institution, the Coloured Affairs Department. She was one of those instrumental in bringing the All-African Convention and the Anti-CAD Movement together in 1943 into a federal body, now known as the Unity Movement of South Africa.

Jane, a graduate teacher, was also a founder member of the New Era Fellowship (a student organization), the Society of Young Africa (a youth organization), and, in 1961, the African People's Democratic Union of Southern Africa (APDUSA). Her involvement in the last led to her being banned for five years in 1961 under the Suppression of Communism Act. She was chairperson at the time of both the Cape Town branch of APDUSA and the Unity Movement working committee.

There were campaigns throughout the 50s against the establishment of the Department of Coloured Affairs. Educationalists involved in the struggle faced victimisation, virulent attacks as not being "fitted to be educators of the youth"* and banning orders for their determined resistance. Disregarding the views of Coloured people themselves, a series of laws were introduced in the 60s entrenching the extension of apartheid to the Coloured community. The Coloured Persons Education Act of 1 January 1964 removed the control of education for Coloured people from the provincial and central government education departments, vesting it in a Division of Education within the Department of Coloured Affairs. The Coloured Persons Representative Council was set up in 1968.

In 1963 Jane left South Africa clandestinely together with the Presidents of the Unity Movement and the All-African Convention, I. B. Tabata and N. Honono, on a mission to seek aid abroad for the Unity Movement. In this capacity, she formed part of a delegation to the Organization of African Unity.

Jane became the official representative of the Unity Movement in Zambia in 1964. She has written and assisted in the preparation of numerous articles and publications, including a pamphlet issued in 1965 on Bantu Education, drawing on her experiences in the struggle against apartheid education.

---

*S. A. Outlook August 1980, p.127.

11

Janub Gool.

Helen Joseph.

HELEN JOSEPH

Helen Joseph is living evidence that the liberation struggle in South Africa knows no distinction in colour or race. It brings together women and men from all sectors of society and all parts of the country in the fight to topple the apartheid system. Despite her advanced age and ill-health, and despite having already spent 15 years of her life under severe restrictions, she was silenced for the fourth time by a banning order in 1980, at the age of 75.

Helen Joseph was born in 1905 in Sussex, England, and educated there. After completing a degree in English at the University of London, she went to India, where she taught for three years at a girls high school.

In 1931, Helen came to South Africa, initially to stay with friends, and decided to stay. She found a teaching job in Durban and in 1932 married a local dentist, Dr. Billy Joseph. After the outbreak of the Second World War she joined the Women's Auxiliary Air Force as a welfare and information officer, giving lectures to the services on political and current affairs. She stayed on in Johannesburg when she was demobilised in 1945, and became director of a community centre in Fordsburg, a white slum in the city. She was studying for a postgraduate diploma in social studies at this time, at the University of the Witwatersrand.

In 1949, on being appointed Supervisor of Community Centres in Cape Town by the National War Memorial Health Foundation, she established and expanded two community centres amongst the Coloured people. It was a period in which she gradually came to understand the need for political action to eliminate the social ills with which she came into daily contact.

Returning to Johannesburg in 1951, Helen took on the job of secretary to the Medical Aid Society of the non-racial Garment Workers' Union in the Transvaal, led by Solly Sachs. After a short period as a member of the Labour Party, she helped to found the Congress of Democrats and later served as its national vice-chairperson. When the Federation of South African Women was formed in 1954, she became its Transvaal secretary and later, its national secretary. Together with Lilian Ngoyi, she played a major part in organizing the 1956 mass demonstration by women against the pass laws.

In December 1956, by this time a listed person under the Suppression of Communism Act, she was arrested for treason and eventually became one of the the two whites in the first group of those accused in the Treason Trial. In 1957, she was placed under bans forbidding her to attend gatherings or to leave Johannesburg. She was detained without charge for five months during the Emergency declared after Sharpeville.

In October 1962, she became the first person to be put under house arrest in South Africa, on a five year order which was duly renewed in 1967. By this time, divorced, she lived alone. She endured ten continuous years of stringent restrictions, denied visitors, confined to her home in Johannesburg for 12 hours every evening and throughout weekends and prohibited from leaving the city for even a brief holiday. She earned a living by continuing to work for the Medical Aid Fund in the clothing industry. To add to the "official" restrictions, she received numerous death threats and insulting phone calls, and her house was constantly raided by the Security Police.

After a major operation for cancer in 1971, the house arrest and banning orders were not immediately renewed. She continued to be listed under the Suppression of Communism Act which meant she could not be quoted. She was also prohibited from holding office in any organization with political connections. Helen nevertheless used the opportunity to launch herself once more into hard political work, speaking throughout the country on anti-apartheid platforms. Throughout the years of restriction she had never given up learning, writing and studying and in 1975, she earned a Diploma of Theology from London University. She was elected a Fellow of King's College, London, that same year.

Helen has been a friend of Winnie Mandela for many years, referring to Winnie as the daughter she never had. In October 1977, she was sentenced to four months imprisonment for refusing to answer security police questions on an alleged visit that she and three other women had made to see Winnie in Brandfort, her place of banishment.

In June 1980, just a few days after the fourth anniversary of the Soweto uprising, Helen was banned once again, under a two year order preventing her from attending or addressing any gatherings.

DEBORAH MABALE

Deborah Mabale Matshoba is a representative of the younger generation of political leaders and activists in South Africa who came to prominence in the 1970s. As one of the organizers in the black consciousness movement, she was active in the South African Students' Organization (SASO), working as a literacy director until SASO was banned with 17 other organizations on 19 October 1977. She herself is currently under a banning order.

Deborah was born in Munsieville, Krugersdorp in 1950. She studied radiography at Baragwanath Hospital and worked at Krugersdorp and GaRankuwa hospitals. In 1971 she was a representative at the World Conference of the Young Women's Christian Association in Ghana. She studied at the University of Zululand in 1972 and later with the University of South Africa (UNISA).

She became increasingly involved in SASO during this time, and in 1976, the year in which massive student uprisings spread throughout the country, she was among the many student organizers detained. A significant part of SASO's work was in utilising the training of its members for the service of the black community, through projects maintained by a core of full-time organizers. Deborah Mabale was a literacy director for projects centred in the urban areas. Students were trained in literacy teaching at various centres, going out into the community to set up classes.

Following periods of imprisonment in July, August and December 1976, she was detained again in February 1977 under Section 6 of the Terrorism Act, one week after her marriage to Gilbert Mabale who was also detained during the year. In all she was held for 18 months in various police stations and jails in Natal and the Transvaal. Finally on 31 August 1978 she was taken to Bethal and told that a warrant for her release had been issued, and then driven to Krugersdorp. However she was not to be reunited with her family but detained under Section 10 of the Internal Security Act. Deborah was finally released in December 1978 and was served with a five year banning order restricting her to Krugersdorp. In February 1979 she was refused permission to attend her belated wedding party.*

*Post, 3.1.79.

WINNIE MANDELA

Among all the courageous women of South Africa, Winnie Nomzamo Mandela is a living symbol of the strength, confidence and vitality of the liberation struggle. Through two decades, she has been a continuing source of inspiration both to those involved in the fight against apartheid inside South Africa itself, and to the worldwide movement of support and solidarity with the oppressed.

Winnie Mandela's last private meeting with her husband Nelson Mandela, leader of the African National Congress (ANC) serving a life sentence on Robben Island, was in March 1961, shortly before he went underground. Three months after their marriage in June 1958, she was arrested for protesting against

Deborah Mabale.   Winnie Mandela.

the extension of the pass laws to women and, despite her pregnancy, spent two weeks in detention. She and Nelson have spent perhaps four months of their married life together.

As a member of the ANC, Winnie Mandela has endured a life of deprivation, isolation and loneliness, constant police persecution, restriction, banishment, house arrest and detention. She continues to face the apartheid regime with calm stoicism, vigour and above all a great sense of humour.

Winnie was born around 1935 and grew up in a rural area. After matriculating in the Cape, she came to Johannesburg in 1953 and gained a diploma in social science. She became the first black medical social worker at Baragwanath Hospital and later worked for four years as a social worker with the Child Welfare Society. Her professional career as a specialist in paediatric social work was interrupted by her arrest in 1958 and subsequent banning and detention.

Winnie joined the ANC in 1957 and became an active member of the Women's League. In January 1963, two months after Nelson had been sentenced to five years imprisonment for organizing a strike and leaving South Africa illegally, she was served with a two year banning order, confining her to the Johannesburg area.

Winnie spent the next 12½ years under continuous banning orders, the terms

15

of which were made progressively more stringent. In May 1969, she was arrested along with 40 others under the Terrorism Act and spent the next 491 days in detention, most of it in absolute solitary confinement. In October 1969 she and 21 other detainees were charged with furthering the aims of the ANC. Despite suffering from a heart condition, she was kept without sleep and continuously interrogated for five days and five nights.

Winnie's only period of freedom lasted for less than a year after her ban expired in September 1975. She threw herself into the political struggle during the crucial events of June 1976 and thereafter, becoming a leading member of the Soweto Black Parents' Association and taking part in the foundation of the Black Women's Federation in 1975.

She was arrested in August 1976 and detained for four months under the Internal Security Act. On her release in December 1976 she was issued with a further five-year banning order, due to expire on 31 December 1981. After being initially restricted to Orlando, she was banished in May 1977 to the small town of Brandfort.

Brandfort is a conservative Afrikaner farming settlement in the Orange Free State, about 30 miles north of Bloemfontein. Winnie, who is unfamiliar with the local African language, is under house arrest at her three-room breeze-block house in the black location. She is confined to the house and yard every night, at weekends and on public holidays, and, together with her second daughter Zinzi, who lives with her, is kept under constant security police surveillance.

She is allowed to be in the company of only one other person at a time, apart from Zinzi, can receive no visitors in her home other than relatives, and is obliged to receive fortnightly Holy Communion sitting in the car of a visiting Anglican priest. She is unable to take up employment and in 1980 had to refuse the offer of a post as the head of the Bloemfontein Child Welfare Society. She sees Nelson for 30 minutes every two to three months, speaking to him by telephone through thick plate glass under police scrutiny. She has otherwise on only rare occasions been granted official permission to leave Brandfort, as for example, when she attended the christening of her grandchild, child of her elder daughter Zeni, in Bloemfontein's Anglican Cathedral.

Winnie herself has described Brandfort as a living grave, calculated to break her spirit. This it has manifestly failed to do. Despite the rigours and deprivations of her situation, official harassment and a continuing series of persecutions for allegedly contravening the terms of her ban, she has involved herself in the local community, opening a clinic at her home and setting up a vegetable garden project to assist black families to be more self-sufficient. As one journalist put it, "she seems almost to be spiritually recharged with each curtailment of her personal liberty . . . To her there is little difference in being banned or unbanned, in prison or not. She feels that every black person is in prison in South Africa, it is only the size of the prison which differs."*

*T 27.6.77.

Winnie Mandela, during her brief period of freedom from banning in 1976, defies apartheid at the funeral of Hector Petersen, the first to be shot dead during the Soweto uprising.   *Photo: Peter Magubane.*

Florence Matomela.

FLORENCE MATOMELA
(1910–1969)

Florence Matomela, described as a woman who gave out "warmth and life like the African sun, full of lively energy and songs, and the cheerfulness of her infinitely generous and splendid personality",* was a victim of the apartheid prison system. She died shortly after being released from a gaol sentence, of diabetes aggravated by neglect, harsh treatment and lack of medical care while in prison.

Born in 1910, Florence became a teacher and the mother of nine children, four of whom died in infancy. In 1950, she led a demonstration against the enforcement of new "influx control" regulations in Port Elizabeth, which ended in those present burning their pass books. She led the first batch of volunteers in the Defiance Campaign in 1952 and spent six weeks in prison for civil disobedience. She was later tried together with other Campaign leaders and received a nine month suspended prison sentence. She went on to become the Cape provincial organizer of the African National Congress Women's League in the mid-50s and a vice-president of the Federation of South African Women.

Florence was among the original 156 defendants in the Treason Trial at the end of 1956, but the charges against her were withdrawn a year later. She continued to be actively involved in resistance to the pass laws, and was arrested

---

*For their Triumphs and For their Tears, Hilda Bernstein (IDAF 1978) p.62.   17

and charged in 1959. In 1962 she was banned and restricted to Port Elizabeth. The following year, she was detained in solitary confinement under the 90-day law.

In 1964, she was among 161 Port Elizabeth residents sentenced to two to three year prison terms for belonging to the ANC. While serving her sentence, in 1966, she and 50 of the other original defendants were brought to court on further charges of promoting the banned ANC, and sentenced to further terms of three to four and a half years. They nevertheless successfully appealed against the sentences and, Florence included, were released at the beginning of 1968. As soon as they were set free, they were served with banning orders, Florence's being for five years from 31 March 1968 — the day her previous ban expired.

While in prison and detention, Florence's health had deteriorated badly. As a sufferer from diabetes, she needed constant medical attention, yet she had sometimes even been deprived of the insulin she needed. In 1965, her husband had died, leaving the couple's five children — yet she was not told of his death by the prison authorities and learned the news only on her release three years later. In June 1969, she herself died of her accumulated health problems.

CHARLOTTE MAXEKE
(1874–1939)

Charlotte Maxeke, a founder of the African National Congress Women's League and a woman of wide-ranging talents in the community, the church and the academic and educational field, was described during her lifetime as "the mother of African freedom" in South Africa.* Aside from her political work, in which she proved a vigorous and outspoken opponent of the South African government over many years, she was at various times a college principal, a teacher and lecturer, a journalist, a prison visitor and probation officer, a social worker, and a widely-known and respected church and community leader.

Within the ANC, Charlotte Maxeke is today remembered as a pioneer and a continuing inspiration for women in the liberation struggle. "Her very participation in Congress activities . . . and in the general struggle of the African people symbolised the determination and willingness of the ANC to involve women and crystallise the belief in our movement in the equality of both sexes."†

Charlotte Maxeke was born Charlotte Makgomo Manye at Ramokgopa in the Pietersburg district of the Cape on 7 April 1874. She received her elementary and secondary education in Uitenhage and Port Elizabeth. In her youth she was an accomplished singer, and travelled to Britain, Canada and the United States in the 1890s with a choral group of which she was a member.

In the United States she was offered an opportunity for university training, and remained behind to study at Wilberforce University, Cleveland, Ohio — a university controlled by the African Methodist Episcopal (AME) Church. While at Wilberforce she developed lasting contacts with the black American

---

18   *Dr. A. B. Xuma, subsequently the President-General of the ANC, at a meeting of the All-African Convention in December 1935.   †*Sechaba*, August 1980, p.26.

community and its leaders. She also met and married Rev. Marshall Maxeke, another South African and like herself a student at Wilberforce. She graduated in 1905, becoming the first African women from South Africa to obtain a bachelor's degree.

Returning to South Africa, Charlotte and her husband together founded the Wilberforce Institute, later to be one of the leading Transvaal secondary schools for Africans. In the years that followed, she became drawn into a wide range of political and community activities, addressing numerous conferences and frequently being called to give evidence before Government commissions dealing with African affairs.

In 1919 she achieved political prominence as a leader of women demonstrators against proposals to extend the pass laws to women. She was instrumental in founding the Women's League of the ANC and served as its President for many years. She became involved in labour issues, giving support in 1920 to early efforts to launch a national trade union movement for Africans. Together with her husband she worked as an editor of a number of African newspapers and was a contributor to a pioneering collection of African biographies published in 1931. She ran an employment agency for African women, became a government proba-tion officer for African juveniles and was a regular visitor to women's prisons in South Africa. Her involvement in the church continued throughout her life and in 1928 she returned to the United States to attend a conference of the AME Church.

South African children are preparing for a new future at the Solomon Mahlangu Freedom College of the African National Congress in Tanzania. This picture shows the Charlotte Maxeke Clinic. *Photo: Eli Weinberg.*

19

FATIMA MEER

Fatima Meer is a long-standing proponent of black unity in the struggle against apartheid. She has combined a distinguished academic career with a position of prominence in the women's movement. An internationally-recognised socio-logist, she is, as senior lecturer at the University of Natal, the highest-ranking black academic in a white South African university. She has managed to retain her position despite legislation excluding blacks from white English-speaking universities and the imposition of a five year banning order in July 1976. At this time, in the midst of the Soweto uprising, she was also the national president of the Black Women's Federation.

Fatima was born in 1929 and grew up in Durban. Educated at the Universities of the Witwatersrand and Natal, her first job on graduating in social science from the latter was with a government community health programme — a post from which she was sacked on the same day as being issued with a banning order.

She joined the staff at Natal University in 1959 initially as a tutor, and has remained with the sociology department ever since, obtaining her MA for a study of suicide in Durban. In 1973 she became the first black president of the Association of Sociologists of Southern Africa. She has published several books and has lectured at many universities in India, the United States and Britain.

Fatima's pursuit of her academic career has gone hand in hand with her involvement in political struggle. She took part in the Defiance Campaign in Natal in 1952 and was issued with a two year banning order that same year. In 1954 she was among the founders of the Federation of South African Women and addressed the inaugural conference on the position of Indian women under apartheid and their resistance to it. While her husband Ismail Adam, a prominent Natal attorney, was under arrest between 1956 and 1958 as a defendant in the Treason Trial, she ran his legal practice in Verulam near Durban, and organized fund raising events for the families of the Treason Trial defendants.

She continued to be an outspoken and forceful opponent of the apartheid state, becoming one of the best-known voices of the black consciousness movement in South Africa. In December 1974 she was a featured speaker at the Black Renaissance Convention. During 1975, she played a prominent role in bringing South African women of all races together in anti-apartheid activities to mark International Women's Year, and in December, she was elected first President of the South African Black Women's Federation.

In July 1976, Fatima was again banned, this time under a five year order — the first known to have been issued under the Internal Security Act — due to expire on 31 July 1981. She was restricted to the Indian area of Asherville, Durban, around her home, prohibited from taking any part in the affairs of the Black Women's Federation, and prohibited from attending political and other types of gathering. While an exemption clause permitted her to retain her job as lecturer at the University of Natal, the order automatically prevented her from publishing her research or being quoted in the press and media. Earlier the same month, she had been refused a passport to enable her to take up the internationally recognised Ginsberg Fellowship in sociology at the London School of Economics and to undertake a six week lecture tour of British universities.

From August to December 1976, Fatima was detained under the Internal Security Act, together with her son-in-law, also a banned person. Prosecutions for breaking the terms of her banning order followed. In August 1978, she was nevertheless permitted to leave South Africa to attend the Ninth World Congress on Sociology at Uppsala, Sweden, a relaxation of the order undoubtedly forced onto the regime by her distinguished academic reputation. Most recently in May 1981, Fatima has set a precedent by challenging the validity and authenticity of her banning order in court.

Fatima Meer.

Florence Mkhize.

One of many demonstrations during the 1950s by women against the pass laws.

21

FLORENCE MKHIZE

"I stand unafraid! I stand defiant! I stand sorry for the Government, its supporters and its puppets."

Florence Mkhize, speaking at a conference organized by the National Union of South African Students, University of the Witwatersrand, September 1980.*

Since Florence Mkhize addressed white South African students during 1980, she has once again been silenced by a banning order. A staunch supporter of the African National Congress, an organizer in the women's movement, community leader and political activist, she has been in the forefront of the liberation struggle for over 25 years.

Florence Mkhize was born in Umlazi, Durban, in 1936, and joined the ANC as a teenager in 1955. She took part in the first demonstration against Bantu Education in 1955, when thousands of people from all over South Africa marched on the Union Buildings in Pretoria, demanding to speak to the Prime Minister Dr. Verwoerd. She became the ANC political organizer in the Natal region at this time.

The following year, 1956, she was the leader of the Natal delegation and the organizer of the ANC Women's League for Natal in the mass demonstration of over 20,000 women against the pass laws. In 1957 she was one of 262 women arrested for protesting against passes outside the Native Commissioner's office in Harrismith.

On 20 March 1960, the day on which the ANC was banned, she was arrested together with Dorothy Nyembe, currently serving a 15 year prison sentence, and detained until June the same year. In 1961 she was again detained as she was preparing to go into hiding; she was later charged and released on acquittal.

Florence was issued with her first banning order in 1962. In the year it was due to expire, 1967, she was arrested for organizing a memorial service for Chief Albert Luthuli, President of the ANC, and served 90 days in prison. In 1968 her banning order was renewed for a further five years.

The restrictions meant much personal hardship for Florence, a seamstress and the sole breadwinner for her family of four children, her husband unable to work through illness. She nevertheless became widely known in the Durban area through her involvement in campaigns around women, education, housing and other issues affecting the local community.

During 1980, over the months leading up to her third and current banning, she gained prominence through her role as Natal provincial secretary of the newly established Women's Federation of South Africa and founder member of the Natal Release Mandela Committee. The Women's Federation became active at the beginning of 1981 in the formation of a national committee to campaign against the state Republic Day celebrations.

Florence's current ban, imposed in February 1981, restricts her to the Lamontville township and the Durban magisterial district.

Post 8.10.80.

IDA MNTWANA
(1903–1960)

Ida Fiye Mntwana was the first President of the African National Congress (ANC) Women's League in the Transvaal and the first national President of the Federation of South African Women on its formation in 1954.

In her address on behalf of the ANC Women's League in the Transvaal at the inaugural conference of the Federation, Ida spoke of the militancy of South African women and their participation in the liberation movement:

"Gone are the days when the place of women was in the kitchen and looking after the children. Today, they are marching side by side with men on the road to freedom. The large attendance at this conference is a clear demonstration of the ground we have already covered. We have come together, women of all races, to co-ordinate our efforts into one great army capable of shaping the future destiny of our children...

"We know that as women we have many problems which hold us back from taking part fully in the struggle, and it is for precisely that purpose that we have come to break down these problems. Let us come out as a united force, let us take our place in the struggle for freedom."

Ida herself was active in the liberation struggle for many years. She became one of the early trade unionists when, as a dressmaker, she joined the Industrial and Commercial Workers' Union in 1927. She was elected to the executive committee of the ANC in the Transvaal in 1953 and was active in the campaigns of that time — particularly against the pass laws and Bantu Education. Ida was one of the organizers of the Congress of the People, in 1955, when the Federation Charter was adopted.

Her colleagues particularly remember her love of music and strong fine voice. Thomas Nkobi, now Treasurer General of the ANC, recalls the moment after the adoption of the Freedom Charter on 26 June 1955:

"The South African police, the army, converged and surrounded the people, the Congress. And of course our people were calm, dignified . . . The people started singing liberation songs and . . . at this time you cannot avoid remembering some of the gallant activists, workers of the African National Congress. I have got in mind here great women like Ida Mntwana. When the police came she started a song and the whole Congress joined in".*

Ida was active in organizing the campaigns against the extension of pass laws to women, that culminated in the historic march on 9 August 1956. She was a defendant in the Treason Trial, until charges against her were withdrawn in December 1957. She died suddenly in 1960.

At the time of her death, ANC meetings and demonstrations were banned. Her funeral became a powerful display of the determination of the movement as thousands of men and women followed the hearse, bearing the colours and wearing the uniform of the ANC.

---

*Isitwalandwe: the Story of the Freedom Charter, (film) IDAF, 1980.

23

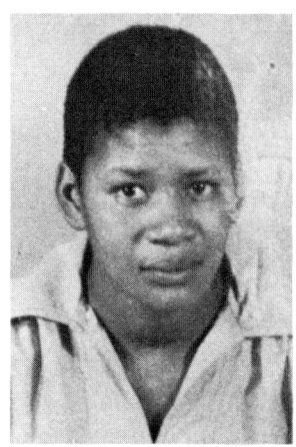

Ida Mntwana, speaking at the inaugural conference of the Federation of South African Women. *Photo: Eli Weinberg.*

Thandi Modise.

THANDI MODISE

The trial of Thandi Ruth Modise, a trained guerilla fighter with the African National Congress, attracted an international campaign of solidarity and focussed attention on the role being played by women in the armed liberation struggle. In November 1980, at the age of 21 and with an eight months old baby girl, she was sentenced to a prison term of eight years under the Terrorism Act. The father of her child was sentenced with her to five years imprisonment.*

Thandi, from Vryburg in the Northern Cape, left South Africa for Botswana in October 1976, in the wake of the Soweto uprising and the country-wide disturbances that followed. At that time she was still a matric student and hoped to obtain a scholarship in exile to further her education. While in Botswana, she joined the African National Congress and opted to undergo a course of military training.

Between October 1976 and January 1978, according to the evidence submitted during her trial before the Kempton Park Regional Court near Johannesburg, she trained as a guerilla in Tanzania and Angola. Besides learning to use a variety of firearms, she told the court she had specialised in sabotage techniques and studied topography, reconnaissance and first aid.

Early in 1978, Thandi returned to South Africa as an underground guerilla fighter. She remained operational for more than a year and a half, before being arrested in October 1979 and detained in solitary confinement. The charges eventually brought against her under the Terrorism Act accused her of undergoing military training with the intention of upsetting law and order in South Africa, and propagating the aims and objectives of a banned organization, the

---

*Thandi's trial was extensively covered in the now banned newspaper *Post* from which this information was obtained.

African National Congress. She was further accused of possessing a machinegun, ammunition and explosives, and conspiring with her two fellow-accused, Moses Nkosi (the father of her child) and Aaron Mogale, to commit arson and sabotage.

Thandi, who was five months pregnant when she was arrested, was refused pre-natal care. She told the court how, following her detention, she underwent interrogation by the Security Branch at the John Vorster Square police headquarters. She was repeatedly hit when she refused to answer questions.

On one occasion she said she was ordered to dig a hole in the ground, given a gun and told to shoot herself. When she refused, a security police captain placed the muzzle of the gun against her forehead and threatened to pull the trigger. .

Thandi said her need for human company while in solitary confinement had almost driven her to suicide. She had been about to kill herself when she felt the baby kicking in her stomach. By the time she was finally brought to court, in April 1980, her child had been born. She explained that she had decided to call the baby Nicolette, after a junior police sergeant who had been the only one to show her any kindness during her solitary confinement and interrogation.

The court also heard from Thandi about the ANC's ideology. She had been taught, she said, not to kill people unnecessarily, but to direct her efforts towards government buildings and installations. The ANC's aim, she said, was for South Africa to belong to all its people, irrespective of colour. Everyone was entitled to enjoy equal rights with no one group dominating the other.

It is believed that Thandi, along with other women political prisoners, may have been moved to Pretoria Central Prison early in 1981. Nicolette is being cared for by relatives.

Students face a Hippo armoured car during the 1976 Soweto uprising. Thandi Modise was one of the thousands of young South Africans who later left the country to continue the liberation struggle.

25

MARY MOODLEY
(1913–1979)

"The government fears my mother because she's a born fighter not a coward. My mother is a courageous woman. She'll never sell her principles at any price. She'll go down fighting, and that is what makes us so proud of her."
Veronica Ally, daughter of Mary Moodley, commenting on the imposition of a fourth five-year banning order on her mother, in April 1978.*

When Mary Moodley died in Benoni Hospital on 23 October 1979, she had become an almost legendary figure, known, loved and respected throughout the East Rand and far beyond. Sixten and a half years of her 66 year life had been spent under continuous banning orders, she had been detained, tortured and imprisoned, forced to give up her job as a garment worker and cut off from friends and political involvement. Yet despite great personal deprivation and sorrow, she had an apparently inexhaustible fund of warmth and compassion for those around her while maintaining her implacable opposition to the apartheid system to the last.

Auntie Mary, as she came to be universally known, was born in the Orange Free State. She became a solid supporter of the African National Congress and played a leading role in the formation of the Congress Alliance and the Defiance Campaign of the 1950s. During this period she was active in the labour movement — as a trade union organizer for the Food and Canning Workers Union in

---

Voice 8.4.78.

Mary Moodley (*centre*) with family and friends.

26

the East Rand and a member of the Witwatersrand Local Committee of the South African Congress of Trade Unions (SACTU); in her immediate community — as a founder member of the South African Coloured People's Congress and active on numerous local committees; and in the women's movement — as a grassroots organizer and executive member of the Federation of South African Women.

Nearly 20 years of victimisation, police harassment and curtailment of her personal liberty commenced in 1960, when she was arrested and detained along with hundreds of others under the State of Emergency. From 1963 up to her death in 1979, she was "free" from the restrictions of banning for a total of three days.

Despite the state's efforts to reduce Mary to a "non-person", her two-room shack in Wattville township became a haven for the destitute, lonely and persecuted. Living on a small military pension with her husband, who died in 1976 having been out of work for the last 10 years of his life through illness, she somehow managed to bring up eight children and care not only for numerous grandchildren but for others who needed a home. She herself suffered from a longstanding heart ailment, diabetes and associated problems of overweight.

Mary Moodley's funeral in Actonville, Benoni, was attended by more than 2,000 people from all parts of the country and was a moving tribute from the African National Congress. The mourners, wearing lapel ribbons in the ANC colours of black, green and gold, punctuated the four hour funeral service with clenched fist salutes, shouts of "Amandla" and the singing of freedom songs. Speaker after speaker from the Azanian People's Organization (AZAPO), the Soweto Committee of Ten, the Benoni Students Movement, the Congress of South African Students (COSAS), the Writers Association of South Africa, the Labour Party and a host of former colleagues and friends, praised Auntie Mary's unyielding spirit and uncompromising fight for the dignity of her people.

"My biggest heartache during those 15 years was not being able to communicate with my friends. Some of them died and I was barred from attending their funerals. There were weddings, but I could not go. I could not enter a factory and this kept me out of a job as a garment worker. I could not enter institutions of learning nor have anything to do with trade unions. I was cut out from the mainstream of life and left to waste away my years all on my own.

"I stood by what I believed in and when I look at the future I have hope that there will be a peaceful transition to a non-racial society, not because the Government want it — its attitudes are tougher now than before — but because of the goodwill of young people. To them, my only advice is not to be afraid to speak up when they see any injustice being committed. That is our best chance".

Mary Moodley, looking back on her life as a banned person and speaking during the three days of freedom before the imposition of her fourth — and final — banning order in April 1978. (*Post* 5.4.78)

27

THENJIWE MTINTSO

Thenjiwe Mtintso is one of hundreds of young South African women who have concluded that their only way of continuing to make an effective personal contribution to the liberation struggle lies in exile. She was a close associate of Steve Biko, whose death in detention in September 1977 was closely followed by the banning of a wide range of political and community organizations associated with the black consciousness movement inside South Africa. Early in 1979, at the age of 29, she fled from South Africa with her five-year-old son, Lumbumba. She was granted political asylum in Lesotho, where she now lives and works with the African National Congress.

One of Thenjiwe's earliest memories, as a 10-year-old, is of running from the police and hiding under a bed from the sound of the gunfire of the Sharpeville massacre. She was the third-born of a very poor family, even by black standards, and was brought up in a shanty town. At the age of 16 she had to leave school for lack of funds to continue her education and worked as a factory hand to support her mother and ailing sister.

In 1971, after studying by correspondence, she gained a place at Fort Hare University. She joined the South African Students' Organization (SASO) and also became active in the Black People's Convention (BPC). In 1973, she left Fort Hare without completing her course, after being accused of involvement in a number of student strikes, and found work as a reporter on the East London *Daily Despatch*.

In August 1976, while she was working in King Williams Town, Thenjiwe was detained under Section Six of the Terrorism Act. Mapetla Mohapi, a colleague and a full-time general secretary of SASO, had died in detention shortly before. Thenjiwe was taken to the Kei Road Police Station and assaulted by Captain R. Hansen, the head of the local Security Branch. At the inquest into Mapetla Mohapi's death, and on various occasions since, she has described how a wet towel was held over her face after she had first been beaten and kicked. The towel was tightened around her neck and pulled until she could not breathe. When she fainted she was doused with water to revive her.

While in detention in King Williams Town and later in the Transkei, she was interrogated for four days at a stretch without food, water, washing or sanitary facilities, and kept in solitary confinement in a dark cell for two weeks. On her release in December 1976 she was served with a five year banning order restricting her to the magisterial district of Johannesburg.

She was detained for a month in March 1977 and again over the period of Steve Biko's funeral later that year. In October she was re-detained in the general clamp-down and banning of black consciousness organizations, and held under the Internal Security Act almost continuously until December 1978.

On her release she decided that her effectiveness within South Africa had come to an end. She crossed into Lesotho early in 1979.

"My son is already a victim of apartheid. He may not understand the intricacies but he understands the basics:- 'They've taken our land and they've forced my mother to leave my grandmother at home and to leave our country.'
"He understands these things even at his early age . . . His father . . . is also a freedom fighter. We have never been a family, the three of us. We have never sat down together and brought up our son as a family. And this my son knows and knows the reasons — Apartheid is not a matter of choice — you are born into it, he was born into it."
Thenjiwe Mtintso, speaking to UNESCO radio, September 1980.

Thenjiwe Mtintso.

SHANTHIE NAIDOO

Shanthie Naidoo is one of the many South African women who are continuing with the struggle against apartheid in exile.

Shanthie's family has a long history of militant resistance in South Africa and is widely known — so much so that the family home came to be called the "People's House". Through more than three generations, Naidoos have been active in protests and demonstrations against apartheid.

Shanthie herself participated actively in the Federation of South African Women (FSAW) and the Indian Congress. As a young woman she worked in the Congress of Democrats (COD) Office in Johannesburg until the COD was banned in September 1962. She then worked at the South African Congress of Trade Unions (SACTU) office until she was banned in December 1963. When the ban expired, she was served with a new five-year banning order confining her to the Johannesburg magisterial district.

At this point, Shanthie decided to leave South Africa, and applied for permission to work in Britain. However, on 13 June 1969, before permission had been granted, she was arrested in connection with a trial of 22 people charged with furthering the aims of the African National Congress (ANC). The defendants

Shanthie Naidoo bids farewell to her mother and other relatives as she prepares to leave South Africa for exile in 1972.   *Photo: R. Botha.*

included Rita Ndzanga and Winnie Mandela, the latter a personal friend of Shanthie's.

Shanthie was detained for 371 days, six months of which she spent in solitary confinement. While still detained she served a month's prison sentence for courageously refusing to give evidence against the 22 trial defendants. She was also interrogated for long periods; an experience she later described:

> "I was forced to stand for five days and nights while they fired questions at me. I lost all sense of time. I only knew it had been five days when they took me back to the cell and the wardress told me what day it was. I also began to lose hold on reality — towards the end of the interrogation I had terrifying hallucinations, like nightmares, in which the questions became all mixed up with broken dreams. I didn't know what was happening . . . "*

On her release in June 1970, a protracted struggle ensued to obtain an exit permit. Only in 1972 was Shanthie finally able to leave South Africa for exile.

Shanthie's grandfather was involved in the passive resistance campaigns led by Mahatma Gandhi in South Africa between 1906–1913. They were aimed at gaining recognition of the rights of South African Indians to remain in South Africa. Her grandfather's admiration for Gandhi's ideals of non-violence led him to give his five sons, including Shanthie's father, Roy, to Gandhi for adoption. The

---

You have struck a rock, IDAF 1980.

boys were brought up on Gandhi's cooperative farm in South Africa and later studied under the Bengali poet Rabindranath Tagore in ashrams in India. Roy returned to South Africa in the 1920s to play a leading role in the Indian Congress and the trade union movement. Shanthie's mother was jailed during the Defiance Campaign.

As children, Shanthie and her brothers and sisters were taken to political meetings and all became involved in the youth section of the Indian Congress. Later, they faced arrest and imprisonment for their commitment to the liberation struggle. Shanthie's brother, Indres, was one of the accused in the first sabotage trial in the Transvaal in 1963 and served a 10-year sentence on Robben Island. Murthie, Shanthie's other brother, was detained under the 90-day Clause in 1964. Her sister, Ramnie Dinat, is also in exile. At the age of nine, Ramnie was arrested for distributing pamphlets in Doornfontein, Johannesburg.

RITA NDZANGA

Rita and her husband Lawrence are both trade unionists who continued to work for a democratic South Africa despite great personal suffering and ultimately — in Lawrence's case — death at the hands of the security police.

In the 1950s Rita was Secretary of the Toy Workers Union and, alongside Lawrence, a leader of the South African Railway and Harbour Workers Union in the Transvaal. Both were active in the South African Congress of Trade Unions (SACTU). Rita assisted at SACTU Head Office during the 1960 Emergency when hundreds of members were arrested and those who escaped detention went underground or into exile. In 1964 she was banned from trade union activities, at a time when open struggle was being increasingly obstructed by the regime.

Rita and Lawrence were among a group of 17 men and five women brought to court on 21 charges under the Suppression of Communism Act in December 1969. During their months of solitary confinement all the detainees were tortured. Rita gave a vivid account of how she had been treated by the security police:

"They dragged me to another room, hitting me with their open hands all the time. . . they ordered me to take off my shoes and stand on three bricks. I refused to stand on the bricks. One of the white Security Police climbed on a chair and pulled me by my hair, dropped me on the bricks. I fell down and hit a gas pipe. The same man pulled me up by my hair again, jerked me and I again fell on the metal gas pipe. They threw water on my face. The man who pulled me by the hair had his hands full of my hair . . . I managed to stand up and then they said: 'On the bricks!' . . . and they hit me again while I was on the bricks. I fell. They again poured water on me . . ."*

The 22 people accused were held for 17 months, during which they were

---

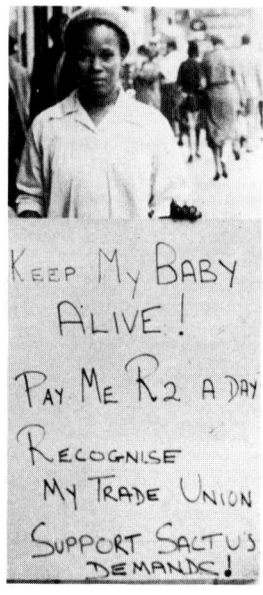

Rita Ndzanga.   Rita Ndzanga by the grave of her husband Lawrence. He died in police custody in 1972.   *Photo: Gamma.*

charged and acquitted twice before being finally released. The four Ndzanga children were without their parents for this period. Both Rita and Lawrence were immediately banned again for five years. The couple were held again under the Terrorism Act in November 1976, the year after their bans expired. On 9 January 1977 Lawrence died in detention in the police cells. On the day after his funeral, Rita was released on bail.

Rita is secretary of the General Allied Workers Union (GAWU) which aims to promote non-racial trade unionism and refuses registration under the new Industrial Conciliation Act.

In 1981 Rita wrote a letter to the press in support of the campaign for the boycott of the regime's Republic Day celebrations:-

> "We the oppressed people have no cause to celebrate when the basic demands of the Freedom Charter have not been given to the people. The system has further intensified our oppression by using some of our own brothers and sisters against us . . . They live like prisoners in those big houses where they have isolated themselves from the community . . .
>
> "What we want is a democratic South Africa where all have a say in making the laws."*

LILIAN MASEDIBA NGOYI
(1911–1980)

"If I die, I'll die a happy person because I have seen the rays of our new South Africa rising."

Lilian Ngoyi, 1974.*

Lilian, "Ma-Ngoyi" as she is known by the people of South Africa, retained confidence in the inevitable victory of the liberation movement right up until her death. Thousands of mourners attended her funeral on Heroes Day, 22 March 1980. Throughout years of enforced silence from banning orders, she had remained a symbol of resistance and inspiration.

Lilian is particularly remembered for her participation in the campaign against the extension of the pass laws to women. As president of the Federation of South African Women and president of the ANC Women's League she led more than 20,000 women in the historic march on 9 August 1956.

Ma-Ngoyi was born in Pretoria. She first became active in the struggle against apartheid as a garment worker and member of the Garment Workers Union (GWU). In 1952 she and her daughter marched with thousands of garment workers to protest against the banning of the Secretary-General of the GWU, Solly Sachs. She participated in the Defiance Campaign and was active throughout the 1950s in the ANC Women's League and the Federation of South African

*Sechaba, January 1980.

Lilian Ngoyi   *Photo: Eli Weinberg.*

33

Women. She also served on the National Executive Committee of the ANC. In 1954 she visited Switzerland, the GDR and a number of other countries on a speaking tour.

Lilian continued to fight against oppression although faced with increasing restrictions. At a conference in 1954 held to organize against rent increases, Lilian asked: "Why must we be afraid of being ejected? We are used to living in shelters in Moroka shacks, in tents. Let us not be disgraced by fear of poverty." In 1956 she was arrested with the other 155 Treason Trialists and placed in solitary confinement for 19 days. She was later detained for five months during the Emergency in 1960.

She was served with a five year banning order in 1961, restricting her from attending gatherings. From October 1962 she was restricted to her house in Orlando, Soweto. The banning order was lifted in November 1972.

Lilian was immediately publicly involved again, attending meetings and inspiring a new generation of fighters. She was able to visit Nelson Mandela and other leaders incarcerated on Robben Island, saying afterwards: "How good it was to meet old comrades whose spirits are great."* In 1975 she was silenced by a banning order which was due to expire on 31 May 1980. She died on 12 March 1980 after suffering from heart trouble and hypertension for some months.

A student who had met Lilian in 1975 said:

"My only regret about Mama Lili's death is that she died when the "sun's rays of new South Africa" were already burning the white racist regime out of its seats; she should have been there to see them eventually being completely burned out."†

DOROTHY NYEMBE

Dorothy Nyembe is the longest serving woman political prisoner in South Africa. She was sentenced in 1969 to a 15 year term under the Terrorism Act, after a political career which had already spanned 17 years of determined and fearless activity with the African National Congress.

Born in 1930 in Natal, Dorothy joined the ANC in 1952 and immediately became involved in the Defiance Campaign against Unjust Laws. She was arrested and served two short prison sentences for passive resistance. She was elected vice-chairperson of the Durban branch of the ANC Women's League and became one of the Natal leaders of the Federation of South African Women when it was formed in 1954. In August 1956 she led the Natal contingent of women to the mass demonstration to the Union Buildings in Pretoria against the extension of passes to women.

Dorothy was a tireless organizer, setting up ANC and ANC Women's League branches throughout Natal. She led women both in rural and urban areas in protests against the beerhall system, the government's housing policies, the pass laws and other symbols of apartheid oppression. She played a major role in organ-

*VOW first quarter 1980.
†*Sechaba*, January 1980.

izing boycotts of potatoes (picked by forced and child labour in the Transvaal) and other consumer goods.

In December 1956, she was one of 18 women among 156 people arrested and charged in the Treason Trial. She spent most of 1957 attending court before the charges against her were dropped. In 1959 she was elected President of the Natal ANC Women's League. After being endorsed out of Durban by the authorities, she turned her attention to mobilisation in the rural areas and in 1962, represented the Federation of South African Women at a conference on labour problems called by the South African Congress of Trade Unions and the Natal Rural Areas Committee.

Further periods of imprisonment followed. During the 1960 State of Emergency she was detained for five months and in 1963, she was sentenced to three years imprisonment for furthering the aims of the ANC. Having also been banned in 1963, she was re-banned in 1968.

In 1968 Dorothy was again arrested, detained with 11 others, and in February 1969 charged in Pietermaritzburg under the Terrorism Act and the Suppression of Communism Act, with harbouring guerillas. She was sentenced a month later to 15 years imprisonment.

Dorothy has served her sentence in Barberton Women's Prison, in Kroonstad, Potchefstroom, and lately, it is believed, in Pretoria Central. Even in prison, she has maintained her spirit of defiance, being charged in 1980 with disobeying prison orders and later going on a hunger strike with three other women political prisoners.* She has won international tributes for her courageous contribution to the liberation struggle, including awards from the United Nations Food and Agricultural Organization and the National Front of the Socialist Republic of Czechoslovakia.

---

* *Post* 8.5.80.

Dorothy Nyembe.

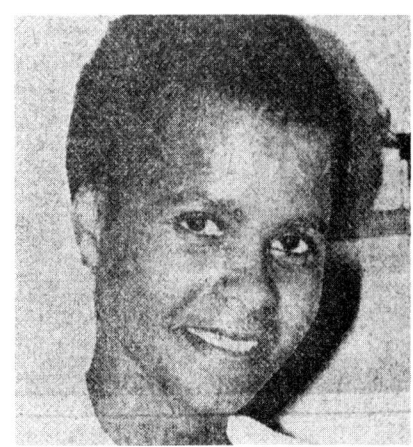

Mamphela Ramphele.

MAMPHELA RAMPHELE

Despite being banned and banished to a remote rural area of the north-eastern Transvaal, Dr. Mamphela Aletta Ramphele has carried on with her medical work among the least privileged sectors of the black community. An Eastern Cape executive member of the Black Community Programme prior to its banning in October 1977, she has played a leading role in developing alternative health and medical facilities to those offered by apartheid.

Mamphela was born in Pietersburg in the northern Transvaal, the third in a family of seven children. Both her parents were teachers and her school environment was dominated by the teachings of the Dutch Reformed church. She studied at the University of the North in the Transvaal and later, while at the University of Natal, became involved with other students in the development of the South African Student's Organization (SASO), the Black People's Convention (BPC) and other black consciousness organizations. Upon qualifying as a doctor in 1972, she served at two provincial hospitals before taking up an appointment at the Methodist Church's Mount Coke Hospital, near King Williams Town, at the beginning of 1974.

In 1975, at the age of 27, she took on the job of superintendent of the newly-established Zanempilo Health Centre at Zinyoka, near King Williams Town. Zanempilo, a project set up by the Black Community Programme, was intended to provide essential health services previously lacking in Zinyoka and other rural areas of the Ciskei bantustan. During the first two years of its operation, it began to tackle the health problems arising from malnutrition, inadequate water supply and sanitation, and rural neglect.

The work at Zanempilo met with resistance from the South African government and the Ciskei bantustan authorities. Mamphela's other political activities also marked her out as a target for security police harassment. She was a trustee of the Zimele Trust, established to help released political prisoners, and a colleague of Steve Biko, killed in detention in September 1977.

In August 1976, Mamphela was arrested at Zanempilo and detained for 139 days under the Internal Security Act.

A banning order followed in April 1977. Under the order, Mamphela was banished to Lenyenye township, a remote community of 4,000 people near Tzaneen in the northern Transvaal, over 600 miles from King Williams Town. She was taken there with no belongings by the security police, without time to sort out her affairs or to arrange for a replacement doctor. In October 1978 her banning order was amended to further restrict her movements, in particular to prevent her from visiting two outstations of the medical practice she had built up in Lenyenye. Hundreds of patients were affected by their subsequent closure.

On two occasions following her banishment and restriction, she was refused permission to pursue a graduate course in tropical medicine, a qualification which would have been particularly relevant to the Tzaneen area.

Despite being unable to take a patient to hospital or fetch medical supplies without first getting permission from the magistrate in Tzaneen, Mamphela has continued with her medical practice, working a 12 hour day at the clinic. She lives in Lenyenye with her mother, her young son Hlumelo and her younger brother.*

*Voice, 11.6.80.

ANNIE SILINGA

In 1954 the crowds gathered on the Grand Parade, Cape Town, heard Annie Silinga declare:

"I will never carry a pass."

Annie has never carried a pass. Although she is now over 70 years old and has been confined to a wheelchair since she suffered a stroke in 1976, she remains as firmly opposed to the apartheid system as when she was active organizing women in the 1950s. Through her own refusal to carry a pass, she has become a symbol of women's resistance to the pass laws.

Annie was born in 1910 at Ngamakwe in the Transkei region. She moved to Cape Town in 1937 to live with her husband and joined the Vigilance Association in Langa to:

"fight for better living conditions for my people . . . which eventually led us to unite under the banner of the now banned African National Congress and organize the Defiance Campaign."*

Annie joined the ANC during the Defiance Campaign and was among the thousands of people arrested. She had walked into a Whites-only waiting room at the railway station with five other women. She was elected to the executive committee of the Federation of South African Women on its foundation in 1954 and was an active member of the ANC Women's League.

While active in political work, she was herself fighting to remain in Langa with her family. In 1956 she was evicted to the Transkei after losing an appeal, but only remained there for a month. She returned to Langa and was sent as a delegate to the historic Congress of the People at Kliptown. Back in Langa, she was arrested again for refusing to carry a pass. The case eventually went to the High Court in Bloemfontein. While her case was in progress, she was among those charged in the Treason Trial. All those charged were later acquitted.

Finally in 1958 the court ruled that she did qualify to remain in the Cape, after she had been living in Langa for twenty-one years. She continued to be harassed for her refusal to carry a pass, and remained active in protests against the pass laws. She was imprisoned again during the Emergency in 1960.

Annie remains committed to a democratic South Africa. In an interview in 1980 she said:

"There are changes all the time but these are not what we want. The kind of changes we want have been spelt out in the Freedom Charter."†

*CT, 28.11.80.
†Ibid.

Annie Silinga (*left*) at a meeting in Cape Town in 1959. Others on the platform are (*left to right*) James la Guma, President of the Coloured People's Congress, Oscar Mpetha, leading member of SACTU and President of the ANC in the Cape, Chief Albert Luthuli, President of the ANC, and Zollie Malindi, a leading member of SACTU and the ANC.   *Photo: Eli Weinberg.*

ALBERTINA SISULU

Albertina Nontsikelelo Sisulu has been under a longer period of continuous banning than any other person in South Africa. At the age of 63, she has spent more than a quarter of her life under orders which restrict her to her home and which have drastically curtailed her social and political activities. She has become internationally known for her courage, fortitude and calm endurance.

Albertina was born in the Transkei and trained as a nurse and a midwife. During the 1940s and 1950s she joined the African National Congress Women's League and became very active both in this and the Federation of South African Women, serving on the first committee and working closely with the ANC Women's League's first President, Lilian Ngoyi. She married Walter Sisulu, who became National Secretary of the ANC and is now serving life imprisonment on Robben Island.

In 1963, together with her 16-year-old son Max, Albertina was arrested and held in solitary confinement under the 90-day law in an atttempt to elicit the whereabouts of Walter Sisulu. He was at that time in hiding, prior to his arrest and subsequent appearance at the Rivonia Trial. On her release, she was elected

38

Provincial President for the Transvaal of the Federation of South African Women.

In 1964, she was issued with her first five-year banning order. When this expired, the ban was renewed for a further five years, with a house arrest amendment confining her to her home in Orlando, Soweto, from 6 p.m. to 6 a.m. during weekdays and all day at weekends. She managed to support herself by working as a nurse. From 1974, the terms of her third banning order were further amended to include public holidays. Under her fourth order, a two-year term issued at the end of July 1979, she was permitted to go to church and the 12-hour house arrest clause was lifted. However, she was still confined to Johannesburg, and could not be quoted, enter a school or factory or take part in any social gathering without special permission. She was also required to apply for permission to visit her husband Walter on Robben Island.*

Throughout her years of banning, Albertina has maintained her home and brought up and educated her own five children and two children of her deceased sister, and cared for seven grandchildren. Her daughter Lindiwe is in exile after being detained for 11 months, tortured and assaulted, following the 1976 Soweto uprising. Her son Zwelakhe, who lives in Orlando and is also a banned person, is President of the Media Workers Association (MWASA) and was news editor of the *Sunday Post* before its banning in January 1981. He himself was detained later that year.†

Post 1.8.79.   †*Focus 33, Mar.-Apr. 1981.*

Albertina Sisulu.

DORA TAMANA

"You who have no work, speak.
You who have no homes, speak.
You who have no schools, speak.
You who have to run like chickens
from the vulture, speak.
Let us share our problems so that
we can solve them together.
We must free ourselves.
Men and women must share
housework.
Men and women must work together in the home and out
in the world.
There are no creches and nursery
schools for our children.
There are no homes for the aged.
There is no-one to care for the
sick.
Women must unite to fight for
these rights.
I opened the road for you.
You must go forward."

Dora Tamana, April 1981*

The words of Dora Tamana provide a graphic insight into the growing strength and vitality of the liberation struggle in the 1980s. Nearly as old as the century, she was a powerful speaker at the inaugural conference of the Federation of South African Women in April 1954. 27 years later, at a conference of the United Women's Organization in Cape Town, attended by more than 400 delegates from the Western Cape, she was again calling on the women of South Africa to unite and mobilise. Through her, those present could look back at what was achieved in the past, and forward along the road of continuing struggle against apartheid.

"Today, we still have our chains" she warned, "but we are not in a trap. We are divided, but we can come together . . . Now that we are strong, call the women, build the organization. Mothers, release yourselves."*

Dora Tamana was born in 1901 at Gqamakwe in the Transkei. When she was 20, her father and two of her uncles were killed in the Bulhoek Massacre, in which 163 people were shot dead by the police.

In 1923, Dora married John Tamana, also from the Transkei. Over the next seven years she bore four children, three of whom died from starvation, tuberculosis and meningitis. The family moved to Cape Town in 1930 in the hope that their children might have a chance to survive. Dora's life continued to be a bleak struggle for basic essentials. Her husband eventually deserted her. She nevertheless became increasingly involved in the wider problems she saw around her, joining the African National Congress and the ANC Women's League, and becoming an energetic organizer in the African and Coloured townships.

During the Second World War, food became scarcer than ever. Various self-help groups sprang up in the townships, and Dora herself decided to set up a creche for 20 babies from six months to five years. She continued to be active in numerous campaigns during the early 1950s against high food prices, Bantu Education, removals and the pass laws, and in the Defiance Campaign.

Dora was sent as a delegate to the inaugural conference of the Federation of South African Women and spoke to the Women's Charter that was submitted to

---

40

the conference. In 1955 she was invited with Lilian Ngoyi to attend a women's peace conference in Switzerland. Together they spent seven months touring Europe, the USSR, China and other socialist countries.

On her return to South Africa, Dora was banned under the Suppression of Communism Act, and suffered constant police harassment for pass law and other "offences".

Dora brought up the five of nine children who survived, ten grandchildren and ultimately a number of great-grandchildren. Through her family, she became personally involved in the armed struggle at an early stage. Her son Bothwell fought Rhodesian and South African troops in Zimbabwe as part of a joint campaign by the ANC and the Zimbabwe African People's Union (ZAPU). He was captured and spent 13 years in the Smith regime's maximum security prisons, only being released following Zimbabwe's independence in 1980.

During the years of UDI, Dora managed to make the hazardous journey to see him and other South African prisoners in jail. At first she travelled on a South African document. After 1976 she was told to apply for a Transkeian passport, and so was no longer able to visit her son. For to have done this would have implied recognition of the "independence" of the Transkei bantustan.

Dora continues to be actively involved in campaigns in the Cape Town area, against high rents and prices, poor housing, inadequate schools, amenities and health services, and other issues affecting the black community.

41

Namibia

LIBERTINE AMATHILA

During a tour of European capitals in 1977, Dr. Libertine Amathila told her audiences about the desperate needs of Namibian refugees in Zambia and appealed for supplies and equipment to build up SWAPO's field medical units. As the only Namibian woman doctor at the time, and SWAPO assistant secretary for health and social welfare, she had been organizing health facilities at the SWAPO health and education centre at Nyango, Zambia, for 1500 women, men and children. Together with a team of trained Namibian nurses, she set up surgeries, a day centre and clinic. When refugee settlements were established in Angola, accommodating over 50,000 Namibians by 1981, she travelled regularly between Zambia and Angola, caring for wounded guerillas, curing illnesses and organizing health education programmes.

Libertine was born at Fransfontein in the north-west of Namibia. She went to school in Okahandja up to Standard 8 and obtained her senior certificate from Wellington School in Cape Town, South Africa.

She became involved in the liberation movement at an early age. She left Namibia in October 1962, when she was 20, determined to become a doctor so that she could play a more effective role in the liberation struggle. She travelled through Botswana, Rhodesia (Zimbabwe) and Zambia to Tanzania, and was awarded a bursary by SWAPO to study medicine in Poland for seven years. After qualifying, she took a post-graduate course in nutrition at the London School of Tropical Hygiene and Medicine, which proved valuable in her work in the refugee settlement in Zambia. After spending three years working in Sweden, she returned to Africa in 1974. She speaks seven languages as the result of her varied experience and training.

In an interview in June 1977 Libertine talked about the deep care she felt about the plight of her people. She described the high morale of people in the refugee settlements despite their lack of most essentials.

"We are not going to put down our arms until South Africa withdraws its troops from Namibia. I am fully convinced our fight is completely a just cause. We have sat for years and years passing resolutions and that has never helped. Nobody enjoys fighting; we all want to live comfortably and peacefully but you come to a point where you have to say enough is enough. We have reached that point. Fighting is a painful necessity for us now."*

Libertine has been particularly concerned with providing community health education and preventive medicine. She contributed papers to the First Congress of the SWAPO Women's Council in 1980, stressing the need for adequate nutrition, sex education and family planning. She is a member of the Central Committee of SWAPO.

---

*Interview published in *The Guardian* (London), 21.6.77.

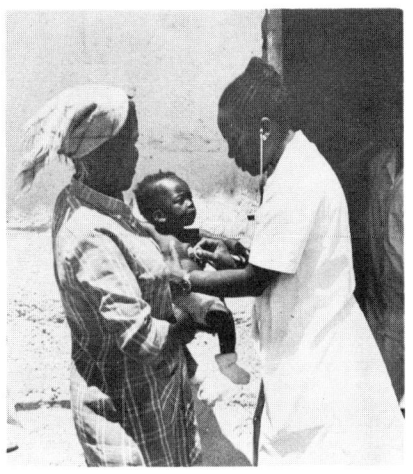

Dr. Libertine Amathila attends to patients at the SWAPO refugee settlement at Nyango, Zambia.

Lucia Hamutenya.

LUCIA HAMUTENYA

As SWAPO's Secretary for Legal Affairs, Lucia Hamutenya has gained first-hand experience of the widespread repression and torture suffered by people in Namibia. She herself has been detained several times and subjected to torture.

Lucia was born in 1952 in Odibo in northern Namibia. She grew up in a family committed to SWAPO. Her father had been detained and interrogated about SWAPO in the early 1960s, and had been flown to Pretoria, South Africa, by the South African security police in 1967 to testify against Herman ja Toivo and 36 others then on trial under the Terrorism Act. He was released after two months, having refused to give evidence. Her brother fled the country in 1962 after protests against Bantu Education. Lucia attended political rallies from childhood and experienced police brutalities at demonstrations and meetings.

Lucia attended secondary school in Windhoek and studied law at Fort Hare University in South Africa. She is one of a tiny number of Namibian women to have a university degree. She was expelled from Fort Hare University and forced to return to Namibia in 1976 when the Soweto uprising resulted in the closure of many schools and universities in South Africa. She completed her studies through a correspondence course with the University of South Africa in 1979.

Lucia, who had joined SWAPO in 1968, started working at the SWAPO national headquarters in Windhoek in 1976, organizing the defence of political detainees and raising funds for bail and to assist the relatives of detainees. She was active mobilising support for SWAPO, especially among Namibian women, going from house to house, handing out pamphlets and addressing rallies.

She travelled widely throughout the country, helping to organize demonstra-

43

SWAPO supporters in Windhoek.

tions and meetings. She was detained for several days in December 1977 at a military camp in Oshakati and questioned about SWAPO's guerilla activities.

Virtually the entire SWAPO leadership inside Namibia were arrested in April 1978. As the only member of SWAPO's national executive still at liberty, Lucia ran the SWAPO office and informed the press about harassment and threats against SWAPO supporters by the DTA.

On 3 December 1978, on the eve of South African-sponsored internal elections in Namibia, Lucia was amongst a large number of SWAPO officials and members to be arrested. She and others were picked up in early morning raids following a demonstration in Windhoek against the elections, where police had beaten up people and taken many to police stations. Her attempts to obtain their release were halted when she was herself detained under the Terrorism Act. She was made to stand in the centre of a room while being questioned about her work in SWAPO and her connections with SWAPO officials in Angola. She was slapped in the face and suffered damaged eardrums as a result. She and other SWAPO leaders were released on 23 December 1978.

During 1979, Lucia was detained twice. Her longest period in detention began in April 1979, when she was detained under Proclamation AG26, together with many other SWAPO officials, and held in solitary confinement at Gobabis prison.

During her detention, Lucia was exposed to psychological pressures during interrogation, resulting in hallucinations, nightmares and fainting spells. She was unable to eat or sleep. She was transferred to Windhoek Central Prison after her condition had become serious, but continued to suffer from hallucinations and nightmares. Although she was seen regularly by a doctor, she was only given tranquilisers.*

After her release from detention on 27 July 1979, Lucia continued her political activities. She organized a rally for Namibia Day on 26 August attended by more than 30,000 people. She travelled to the north of the country, collecting evidence about the disappearance of SWAPO supporters and taking affidavits on torture from victims and their relatives. At the end of 1979 Lucia left Namibia for exile after further police harassment and questioning.

---

*Interview with IDAF in London, February 1980, and written communication, May 1981.

IDA JIMMY

An experienced SWAPO activist in the Lüderitz area, Ida Jimmy was sentenced, at the age of 35, to seven years imprisonment under the Riotous Assemblies Act and Section 3 of the Terrorism Act. Her arrest followed a speech she made at a SWAPO rally in Lüderitz on 13 July 1980.

In her address to the 200 people at the rally, Ida accused the South African Defence Force of shooting innocent people without warning and presenting corpses of black members of the South African armed forces as those of SWAPO combatants. She urged people to give shelter and food to SWAPO guerillas, and stressed that they were the sons and daughters of the Namibian people.

Ida pleaded not guilty to the charge of inciting or encouraging people to harbour or aid SWAPO guerillas, but admitted that she had addressed a public meeting of SWAPO.*

At the time of her trial in October 1980, she was seven months pregnant. She gave birth to a baby boy in prison in December.

Ida Jimmy was born at Valgraas in southern Namibia. She has four children and two other dependants. Because of her political activities, she was sacked from her job in Lüderitz and was unable to find employment. She became active in the Lüderitz branch of SWAPO in 1974, and was elected chairperson of SWAPO Women's Council, Lüderitz branch in 1977.

Her outspoken criticism of South Africa's illegal occupation of Namibia resulted in her first arrest on 27 April 1979, together with her four-month-old baby boy, Natangwe. She was one of approximately fifty top officials and senior members of SWAPO arrested at the time under a law promulgated the previous year to allow for arrest and indefinite detention without charge or trial, Proclamation AG26. During her imprisonment, Ida and others were held in solitary confinement and were prevented from communicating with relatives or friends. She participated in a hunger strike in protest against these conditions, and to commemorate the anniversary of the Kassinga massacre a year earlier. There were fears that her baby would suffer physical and psychological damage from being kept in a violent prison environment.

Following her conviction after her second arrest and trial in 1980, Ida was held in Windhoek Central Prison pending an appeal. She is likely to be sent to Kroonstadt Women's Prison in the Orange Free State or another prison in South Africa, where she will suffer the additional hardship of separation from her country, family and friends.

As the only Namibian woman known to be serving a prison sentence under South African security laws for her political beliefs, Ida has become a symbol of the many women fighting for the freedom of their country from South African rule.

---

*FOCUS 34 May-June 1981, drawing on transcriptions of Ida's speech and subsequent statements.

45

Gertrude Kandanga.

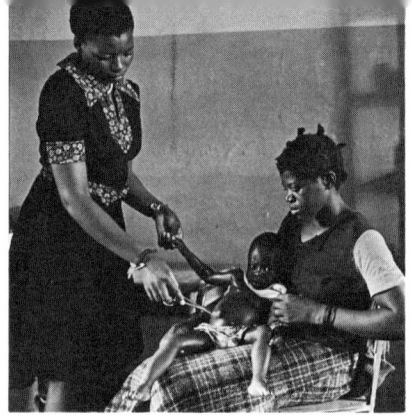

The SWAPO Women's Council is developing preventive health services in exile. A clinic at the Namibian Health and Education Centre, Kwanza Sul, Angola.
Photo: Joost Guntenaar/AABN.

GERTRUDE KANDANGA

Described as a brilliant speaker who has encouraged many women and men to actively participate in the liberation struggle, Gertrude Kandanga was one of the first women among SWAPO activists and leaders to speak on SWAPO platforms and to mobilise the Namibian people.* She became involved in political activities in 1959, and addressed numerous meetings and held official positions in the liberation movement. From 1969 to 1979 she was chairperson of SWAPO Women's Council, Walvis Bay branch.

At a public meeting in Oshakati in October 1977, when Gertrude was on a platform with other SWAPO leaders protesting against the emergency regulations in force in Namibia and against South Africa's attempts to entrench tribal and racial divisions in the country, she declared:

"SWAPO is fighting for the liberation of all Namibians. We will liberate the suffering masses as well as the whites. Even the young racist South African soldiers, they will be relieved from their unbearable burden so they can go home."†

Gertrude, who was born in 1937 at Omaruru in western Namibia, has five children, three now in exile. Her active political involvement has made her well-known to the South African security police. She was arrested in January 1980 at a police road block between Walvis Bay and Swakopmund, while on her way to address a public meeting in Swakopmund that day. She had been expected to attend the First Congress of the SWAPO Women's Council in Angola the following week. The Congress elected her Deputy Secretary in her absence.

Gertrude spent a year and three months in detention without charge or trial. She became seriously ill, suffering from asthma and high blood pressure. She was released in May 1981, and placed under house arrest.

---

46   *Information supplied to IDAF by Axel Johannes, SWAPO Administrative Secretary inside Namibia, May 1981.   †*Namibia Today* (SWAPO), Vol. I, No. 2, 1977.

ELLEN MUSIALELA

"We want to mobilise our women, to make them understand that if women don't cooperate together and fight with SWAPO, then we will never be allowed to be free in any way, because the system we live under, the apartheid regime of South Africa, separates women from men.
"One, we are oppressed as black people, both men and women, and two, as women."*

Ellen Musialela, 1981.

Ellen Musialela, Assistant Secretary for Finance of the SWAPO Women's Council, decided to participate in the liberation struggle in 1964 when she was 14 years old. She later spent seven years in the military wing of the liberation movement as a nurse, until the effects of a snake bite obliged her to give up the work. She has since worked in the political field, and is on the Central Committee of SWAPO Women's Council.

Ellen became aware of racial discrimination as a child, observing the lack of education and of transport for black children, and decided to join SWAPO. She began organizing amongst students, travelling to different parts of Namibia and encouraging students to join the liberation movement.

On her return from a fund-raising trip with a colleague to Botswana in 1963, she and her companion found that they were wanted by the police as "terrorists". They immediately set off again for Zambia and permanent exile, narrowly escaping being caught by South African soldiers.

Once in exile, Ellen began working as a military nurse with SWAPO. She found many women in the People's Liberation Army of Namibia (PLAN) holding responsible positions as commanders in the battlefield, in communications, logistics or as organizers. Women were assigned the same duties as men.

Ellen has been working actively in the SWAPO Women's Council which was formed in 1969. She has made broadcasts, attended conferences and talked about women's plight inside Namibia. As a result, many women have joined the liberation struggle. She found that many women from inside Namibia lacked self-confidence "because the enemy made a point of depicting women as less than nothing, just something to be pushed into the kitchen and stay there."† When they came into exile and participated in the SWAPO Women's Council, they gained political awareness and were keen to become active in many fields.

In January 1981, Ellen completed a fund-raising tour of the United States to gain support for a number of projects for women in the refugee settlements. The women need equipment for a maternity clinic, books and other materials for a literacy campaign, and funds for an agricultural cooperative.

---

* *Women's Fightback*, (London) February 1981.
†*Anti-Apartheid News* (London) March 1981.

RAUNA NAMBINGA

Rauna Nambinga's experiences illustrate the harsh manner in which the South African police and army treat civilians in Namibia.

Rauna, a trained nurse who was born in 1950 at Okadiva in northern Namibia, was twice arrested, in 1975 and in 1980. Each time she was tortured, ostensibly for giving medicine and money to SWAPO guerillas. She described her experiences to the International Commission of Inquiry into the Crimes of the Racist and Apartheid Regime in Southern Africa, at its meeting in Angola in January 1981.*

On 17 September 1975, Rauna was working at Engela, a Finnish Mission Hospital, when she was arrested by members of the South African security police and taken to a detention centre at Ogongo. Her arrest took place at a time of large scale police operations against SWAPO members.

Rauna was interrogated for seven days by police, who asked her if she gave medicine and money to SWAPO guerillas. When she denied this, she was beaten with rifle butts, exposed to the sun for long periods, and hung from the roof by a rope tied to her arms behind her back.

She was transferred to Ondangwa prison on 24 September 1975, where her ordeal continued. She was kept in solitary confinement in a cell which contained one blanket and a bucket. She remained there until the first week in November, and was called once or twice per week to the office for further interrogation. Each time she was beaten and forced to agree that she had helped SWAPO guerillas.

From Ondangwa, Rauna was transferred to Windhoek Central Prison where She was held in solitary confinement throughout November, sometimes without being given food or drinking water for three days at a time.

On 1 December 1975, she and five other SWAPO members — Aaron Muchimba (SWAPO Treasurer and National Organizing Secretary in Namibia), Hendrik Shikongo, Andreas Nangolo, Naemi Nambowa and Anna Ngihondjwa (the last two also nurses from Engela Hospital) appeared before the Windhoek Supreme Court charged under the South African Terrorism Act with being members or active supporters of SWAPO and taking part in "terrorist activities aimed at overthrowing the lawful administration of South West Africa". Ruana was accused of crossing into Angola to meet a group of SWAPO members and giving them goods and money.

Called to give evidence, Rauna told the court that she had joined SWAPO in 1973 after attending a meeting at Engela that had stirred her. She found that SWAPO rejected apartheid and the homeland policy and stood for a single unitary state. It was fighting for the interests of the people and for Namibia's liberation. Rauna described her crossing into Angola with her brother to distribute food and goods to people who had fled across the border to escape from the effects of apartheid, floggings and repression.

On 12 May 1976, she was sentenced to seven years imprisonment. Death

*FOCUS Special Issue No. 2, April 1981.

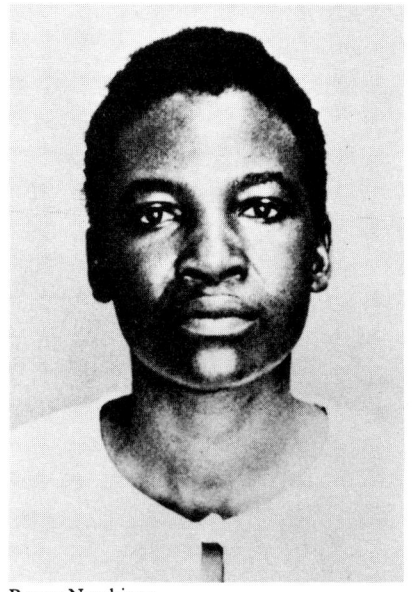

Rauna Nambinga.   Nahambo Shamena.

sentences were imposed on Shikongo and Muchimba. Rauna was transferred to Windhoek prison at the conclusion of the trial and later to Kroonstad Women's Prison in South Africa.

Serious irregularities were discovered in the conduct of the trial, which led the Appellate Division of the Bloemfontein Supreme Court to set aside the death sentences and to cancel the prison sentences. Rauna was released and returned to work at Engela Hospital.

She was again arrested on 15 July 1980, taken to Oshakati prison and asked to give details of assistance given to SWAPO. She was again severely tortured, given electric shock, and hung by a rope from the roof. She was beaten so severely by police that a doctor at the military hospital found that her head was seriously injured, her eardrums had burst and her left kidney was also injured. She continued to be tortured, subjected to assault and attempted rape.

On 10 November 1980, she was taken to Swakopmund and told to work in a supermarket. She was regularly visited by the police, and pressured to act as an informer and agent. She refused.

On 24 December 1980, Rauna decided to run away from Swakopmund, and succeeded in making her way to Angola. In January 1981, she gave evidence in Luanda to the International Commission of Inquiry.

She told the Commission that she was still unable to hear properly with her left ear, that her head remained numb and that she had continual pain in her ribs and chest on the left side.

NAHAMBO SHAMENA

Nahambo Shamena, a teacher, remembers the forced removal of black people from the old location in Windhoek to Katutura, in 1959. "The women who were at the old location protested about being moved to Katutura. That was terrible because they knew if they were moved further away it would cost them a lot. A lot of women were beaten by the police when they refused to move there."*

Nahambo trained as a teacher in 1953 when she was 19 and began teaching at Ongwediva in northern Namibia. She came to abhor the system of Bantu Education which gave black children an inferior education.

As teachers and as SWAPO members, Nahambo and her husband opposed Bantu Education. They protested against the tribal policies imposed on the country by South Africa, gave shelter to SWAPO members in hiding, and organized meetings and demonstrations.

In 1973, Nahambo became internationally known when she wrote a letter to the United Nations Secretary General, Dr. Waldheim, describing the situation in Namibia. Her husband had been arrested for the second time, and was being held under harsh conditions, together with other SWAPO members. Nahambo had gone with him and others to organize a boycott against the Bantustan elections due to take place in Ovamboland. Her husband was arrested shortly afterwards.

The prisoners were held in Oshikango prison, frequently without being given food or water. The wives of the prisoners found ways of communicating with them by walking past the prison and shouting and singing information about events at the United Nations and other news. One day, Nahambo heard a hoarse voice whispering: "Go and write to the United Nations, the South Africans are killing us here". She managed to see her husband and take him food, and was appalled by his condition. She wrote a letter to the United Nations, sending it through underground contacts. The letter was endorsed by the Organization of African Unity and by SWAPO, and was published in full.

When her husband was released from detention, he fled into exile. Nahambo remained with her six children but fled to Zambia in July 1974 after being told by friends that police were about to arrest her because of her letter to Dr. Waldheim. Her children had to be left behind in the care of relatives.

In November 1974, Nahambo was appointed Head of SWAPO Women's Council, a position she held until December 1975. She was the Representative of SWAPO Women's Council in Britain until 1980 when she went to study in Roumania, where her husband is the official SWAPO representative. She attended the First Congress of SWAPO Women's Council in Angola in January 1980.

*Interview with Nahambo Shamena, February 1980, by A. Murray Hudson.

The SWAPO Women's Council places a high priority in developing education schemes in exile, to enable women to participate fully in Namibia's reconstruction. *Photo: Joost Guntenaar/AABN.*

SWAPO aims at self-sufficiency in its refugee settlements. An agricultural co-operative at the Namibia Health and Education Centre, Kwanza Sul, Angola. *Photo: Joost Guntenaar/AABN.*

All sections of the community are involved in the continuing struggle for liberation. A SWAPO rally inside Namibia.

"After independence, the Namibian women have nothing to lose, but everything to win. They have an important role to play in the transition from the old, decaying social order, colonialism and capitalism, to a new democratic social order." — Lucia Hamutenya.

"The SWAPO Women's Council has succeeded in drawing thousands of women into our liberation activity. This liberation activity is itself an important process of learning. It has exposed thousands of Namibian women to many new ideas which are revolutionizing their world outlook." Netumbo Nandi, Chief Representative of SWAPO in East Africa and member of SWAPO Central Committee.

25 Years on

The majority of the South African women whose lives are described in this book took part in the historic 1956 demonstration against the pass laws. They were prominently involved in the freedom struggle at a stirring stage in the growth of the liberation movements, before the banning of the African National Congress and the Pan-Africanist Congress. With the exception of some who have since died, they continue as energetic fighters and respected leaders in the 1980s. Meanwhile, thousands of others, most of whom must remain anonymous, have taken up their banner throughout Southern Africa.

Today, women in South Africa and Namibia are playing a central role in the liberation struggle, including armed guerilla action directed at the military and state machinery. Over the 25 years during which South African Women's Day has been celebrated, the resistance inside both South Africa and Namibia has expanded dramatically. All sectors of the oppressed have become involved in campaigns against low wages and discriminatory working conditions, Bantu Education, the lack of health and social services in both rural and urban areas, slum housing and exorbitant rents, the application of pass laws, forced removals and evictions, and many other aspects of apartheid.

Workers on strike at the Heinemann Electric plant in South Africa. They were attacked shortly afterwards by police wielding long wooden sticks.

The women at Crossroads squatter camp were supported throughout South Africa and internationally in their struggle to remain in Cape Town to seek work and to live with their families. Their determination won a temporary reprieve from the regime in December 1978.

Photo: IFL.

53

Opposition to high rents for inadequate housing is becoming increasingly well-organized. In September 1980 the Women's Federation of South Africa (WFSA) led a march on the Soweto Community Council, in protest at rent increases.

Friends and supporters of the "Pretoria Twelve", African National Congress members on trial under the Terrorism Act, demonstrate outside the court in June 1977.

"And when they come to demolish Crossroads, what will the women do? We are not going to move here in Crossroads. We are going to stay and build our houses again. They can take guns and shoot us . . . We are not prepared to move. We don't want to move."
women from Crossroads.

54

Women in Prison

As part of its humanitarian work, the International Defence and Aid Fund has supported campaigns for the release of political prisoners in Southern Africa.

Convicted women political prisoners in South Africa — including those from Namibia — are most commonly held in Barberton Prison in the Transvaal, Kroonstad Prison in the Orange Free State or Potchefstroom Female Prison in the Witwatersrand. At the beginning of 1981, however, reports filtering out of South Africa suggested that all women political prisoners had been transferred to Pretoria, in a security move apparently prompted by a series of hunger strikes and other protest actions by prisoners at both Kroonstad and Potchefstroom.

Women political prisoners receive harsh treatment. Like their male counterparts on Robben Island and in Pretoria Prison, they are allowed no remission of their sentences but must serve the full term, and they are kept separate from other prisoners.

Women prisoners are believed to have been subjected to a total ban on study rights and newspapers, and their reading material restricted to women's magazines and non-political material. This contrasts with the authorities' treatment of male prisoners, who won back their study rights in 1980 following a campaign both inside South Africa and internationally.

The women are also deprived of physical recreation. Washing clothes appears to be the main form of work allocated to them, although at Kroonstad in the past they are known to have also undertaken gardening and housework. Their isolation from the outside world is accentuated by the difficulties and obstruction which relatives face in locating and visiting them in prison. One woman sentenced in 1979, for example, is believed to have received only one visitor during the first two years of her sentence.

DOROTHY NYEMBE, THANDI MODISE and **IDA JIMMY** (listed above) are three among a total of 15 women political prisoners known to be serving sentences in South African jails in 1981. The others are:-

FEZIWE JOSEPHINE BOOKHOLANE (BURULANI), a nursing sister aged about 40, sentenced in April 1979 under the Terrorism Act to eight years imprisonment. She and five others were alleged to have recruited 75 young men and women for military training abroad with the ANC. She is the stepmother of Thabani Bookholane, one of the 12 ANC members murdered by South African commandos during a raid on residences in Matola, Mozambique, in January 1981. Her husband, "Fats" Bookholane, is a well-known Johannesburg actor.

ELIZABETH GUMEDE, aged in her late 50s sentenced in June 1979 to five years imprisonment under the Terrorism Act. Together with her niece, Montshidisi Serokolo (*see below*), and Montshidisi's mother (who was acquitted), she was accused of harbouring and assisting guerillas by giving them food, money and accommodation. She comes from Soweto.

PAULINE LEKHULA, a Soweto student born in 1955, sentenced to five years imprisonment in November 1976 under the Sabotage Act, for setting fire to a railway station ticket office in the aftermath of the Soweto uprising.

CAESARINA MAKHOERE, a student in her 20s, sentenced to five years imprisonment under the Terrorism Act in 1979.

MAGOTAKE ESTHER MALEKA, born in 1943 in the Transvaal, sentenced to five years imprisonment in December 1976 under the Terrorism Act for recruiting two men for guerilla training outside South Africa with the ANC. She was held in solitary confinement from March 1976 up to the time of her trial. She has two children, and, up to the time of her arrest, also acted as guardian and breadwinner for six younger brothers and sisters.

THANDISO MANGUNGO, sentenced to five years imprisonment under the Terrorism Act in 1979, when she was 19.

HAPPY JOYCE MASHAMBA, born in 1950, a library assistant at the University of the North, Turfloop, Transvaal, prior to her arrest in 1976. She was sentenced in June 1977 to five years imprisonment under the Terrorism Act for being a member of the ANC and furthering its aims by recruiting guerillas. Her husband, Tintiswalo Mashamba, a philosophy lecturer at the University of the North, was also sentenced to five years imprisonment at the same trial and is on Robben Island. The couple have two young children.

ELIZABETH NHLAPO, serving a five year sentence since March 1979 or before for her political activities.

ZODWA ELIZABETH NTOMBI, sentenced to five years imprisonment in early 1979 for recruiting others for military training.

MONTSHIDISI KATE SEROKOLO, aged 28 and pregnant at the time of her trial in 1979. She was sentenced to five years imprisonment under the Terrorism Act, together with her aunt, Elizabeth Gumede (*see above*). She comes from Mahwelereng, Potgietersrus.

ZANDISILE TSIKI, a student from Port Elizabeth, sentenced to five years imprisonment in February 1977 under the Sabotage Act, when she was 25. The charges related to incidents in the New Brighton township, Port Elizabeth, during the 1976 uprisings.

XOLISE ZEPPE (SEBE), sentenced to seven years imprisonment (two suspended) in May 1978 on conviction of public violence. She was part of a group of 13 teenagers charged originally with the murder of two policemen after the funeral of Steve Biko in September 1977. She was 19 at the time of her trial.

This list may well be incomplete. South African press reports of trials (from which much of the information above is taken) are frequently ambiguous or inconsistent in detail. In particular, the sex of defendants can be unclear. Those under the age of 18, for example, are simply described as "youths" or "juveniles".

Publications by
IDAF in cooperation with the
United Nations Centre Against Apartheid

WOMEN UNDER APARTHEID (1981)   £3.00
120pp. 100 photographs with text.
(ISBN 0 904759 45 8)
This book shows how African women under apartheid are oppressed as black people, as workers and as women. It shows too their part in the struggle for freedom.
The 100 photographs are derived from a photo exhibition commissioned by the United Nations especially for the World Conference of the United Nations Decade for Women in 1980.

WOMEN UNDER APARTHEID (Exhibition)   £5.00
Produced especially for the United Nations World Conference on Women in 1980.
14 display sheets 25 × 17½ inches (63 × 44 cms)
'A fascinating variety of photographs and an excellent text deal with the triple oppression that black women in South Africa are subjected to—as women, as black people and as workers.'   *MORNING STAR*
This portable exhibition illustrates the conditions under which the majority of South African women live today.

CHILDREN UNDER APARTHEID   £2.50
120pp. 110 photographs, with text.
(ISBN 0 904759 31 8)
The most casual glance through this book reveals the suffering apartheid causes . . . *Children Under Apartheid* deserves careful and caring reading.
                          NETWORK (United Society for the Propagation of the Gospel)
The reality of apartheid is vividly shown in a superb collection of photographs. *TRIBUNE*

CHILDREN UNDER APARTHEID (Exhibition)   £4.50
Available in English, French, German and Spanish editions
12 display sheets 25 × 17½ inches (63 × 44 cms)
Excellent for display.   *THE AFRICA FUND, USA*
This superb photo set not only illustrates the appalling conditions of black children under apartheid, but also captures their spirit of defiance and resistance.
                                                        ANTI-APARTHEID NEWS

SOUTHERN AFRICA: Freedom and Peace   £1.50
Addresses to the United Nations 1965-1979.
by Canon L. John Collins (1980), 68pp.
(ISBN 0 904759 33 4)
The Canon has campaigned consistently to rouse the British public and the internationally minded community to the dangers involved in white oppression within Southern Africa.   *AUEW JOURNAL*
These speeches concern the work of IDAF from 1965-1979. But Canon Collins has been involved in active opposition to apartheid and all forms of racism since 1948.

PRISONERS OF APARTHEID   £3.00
A biographical list of political prisoners and banned persons in South Africa
by IDAF Research, Information and Publications Dept. (1978). 180pp.
(ISBN 0 904759 24 5)

Available from International Defence and Aid Fund for Southern Africa,
Publications Dept., 104 Newgate St., London EC1A 7AP.
A complete list of publications is available on request.

Printed in England by A G Bishop & Sons Ltd, Orpington, Kent.

On August 9th 1956, twenty thousand women marched on Pretoria in opposition to the extension of the pass system to women. IDAF has produced this book, in cooperation with the United Nations Centre Against Apartheid, as a tribute to the women of South Africa and Namibia on the occasion of the 25th anniversary of that historic event, commemorated ever since as South African Women's Day.

The women in this book have played leading roles in the struggle for freedom in South Africa and Namibia and although many of them have suffered imprisonment, torture and banning they continue the fight for the liberation of their countries.

International Defence and Aid Fund for Southern Africa
104 Newgate Street, London EC1A 7AP.

£1.00